HOW TO STAY BROKE
SELF-REALIZATION

LANCE OTT

Copyright © 2020 Lance Ott.

All rights reserved. No part of this book may be reproduced, stored, or transmitted by any means—whether auditory, graphic, mechanical, or electronic—without written permission of the author, except in the case of brief excerpts used in critical articles and reviews. Unauthorized reproduction of any part of this work is illegal and is punishable by law.

ISBN: 978-1-68471-669-2 (sc)
ISBN: 978-1-68471-668-5 (e)

Because of the dynamic nature of the Internet, any web addresses or links contained in this book may have changed since publication and may no longer be valid. The views expressed in this work are solely those of the author and do not necessarily reflect the views of the publisher, and the publisher hereby disclaims any responsibility for them.

Any people depicted in stock imagery provided by Getty Images are models, and such images are being used for illustrative purposes only. Certain stock imagery © Getty Images.

Lulu Publishing Services rev. date: 12/27/2019

CONTENTS

Chapter 1   Flat Pockets 1
Chapter 2   Excuses Excuses 5
Chapter 3   False Dreams 9
Chapter 4   Untapped Potential 13
Chapter 5   Debt and Credit 17
Chapter 6   Budget and Spending 21
Chapter 7   Social Status 25
Chapter 8   People Pleaser 29
Chapter 9   Rainy Day Funds 33
Chapter 10   Social Life 37
Chapter 11   Disorganization 41
Chapter 12   Over Night Success 45
Chapter 13   Role Models 49

About the Author 53

Everyone has an excuse it is the downfall of the human ambition, to most, it is so much easier to sit back and watch another person make their dreams happen and wonder why it has not happened for themselves. I too have been a victim of this cancerous mind-state. But like myself one day you will wake up and understand that you have a higher purpose maybe it's to educate maybe it's to entertain maybe it's to motivate whatever the reason for your greatness to be awakened you will know that this is the reason for your existence.

CHAPTER 1
FLAT POCKETS

Why is it easy to spend money, but it is so difficult to keep money in a constant flow to support yourself or your family? How many times have you picked something up and thought, do I really need this? Only because the price was out of budget. Are you not tired of saying to yourself maybe I will get it next time when I have more money?

You have this constant desire in you to want more but not a desire to do the things that put you in a position to obtain more. No one should go after financial freedom thinking that it will bring happiness because it will only make it the more difficult to find, instead find yourself to show why you have accepted the way you have previously lived.

Once you find yourself and learn how to self-motivate nothing will seem impossible nor improbable, but this is easier said than done. It might take a bit of motivation from an outside party, which is completely fine but be wary that this motivation is for the right reasons and that all intentions are to benefit you first. Naturally, the goal is always take care of your family but you cannot take care of anyone if you fail to take care of yourself first. Self-preservation and Self-deprecation are the keys to Self-elevation along with Self-motivation there will be nothing that can stand in the way to your ultimate goal.

Not having any money can be the worst feeling but not having the ambition to change that can be an even worse feeling possibly having long term effects for you and your family's futures. If you are not motivating yourselves to fill those pockets then you are internally and subconsciously fighting your own ambition to be the great person that you knew you could become.

Changing your perception on how you portray yourself can be decisive or detrimental even to how others will depict you as a go getter or just another uninspired person letting the days past. Ultimately it's the choice you make and only YOUR choice to make. The question you have to institute yourself would be, is this the life you want to live or do you feel deep in your heart that you are worth more and deserve more? If the answer is yes then you know what you have to do. 1. Make a plan. 2. Review your plan. Then, 3.Execute the plan It's the only way to reach the goals that you set for yourself and never let that little voice of negativity detour or deter your thought process to financial freedom.

CHAPTER 2
EXCUSES EXCUSES

One thing about making a life for your self is finding a way to get past all of your fears in failure. People will find every excuse in the book of Excuses; they will say things like "I'll wait till the next time I get money" or, "It's not the right time" and, maybe to wait until next season. They will use race as an excuse, oh! They will never buy a product from a person of color all they see is danger when they look my way. Then, there is the subcutaneous age barrier where they say there too old to start something or a product is for a younger crowd when in fact age is universal.

People find it is a lot easier on their conscience to justify why they want to keep the same life. They will even go as far to use children as an excuses to say they don't have the time when in reality, they never make the time. Finding reasons not to begin a journey in bettering your life can be detrimental to not only your health, but also your wellbeing and if you have children, it is taking effect on them as well. Your ability to survive on your own always depends on your sense of restraint or dependency to use excuses. Having a person to bail you out of trouble whether it be financially, or being in judicial trouble, can also have a hindering effect, in the way you perceive thing. That person being your safety net and giving you a sense of security can actually be dismantling you on the account that no matter what happens, you always have a net to catch you if you fall and that will never be a good thing for the independent mentality. Having independence in the success you find valuable will eliminate your thought for making excuses. Just for the simple fact that there is no one to blame for your wrongs. Whenever you do approach incursion, then you will be ready with a plan b, and maybe a plan c, because you know all the responsibility is on your shoulders and the feeling of self-satisfaction is one of a kind.

CHAPTER 3
FALSE DREAMS

Sometimes, and all too often, people fall into the trap of a basic 9-5 job that slowly eats away at what people really want, and that is financial freedom. Aspirations and concrete plans dwindling away as the promise of financial stability is thrust upon you with false dreams of promotions and high wage raises just to be two years in the company and get hit with a "At will" termination contract. Which states that if your employer does not like you, they can terminate you at any time they feel, with no explanation or precautions of early disciplinary actions. Within these false dreams, people become too cheap or afraid to take a leap for their own financial gain, because they are suck in the monotony of "staying above water". Which is just a way of trying to justify struggling on a weekly, maybe even daily basis.

We have all been victims of subconscious programming where we don't realize the terrible habits that we attain over the years and it's not just from adulthood. It starts with us watching our parents as kids just barely making it by, thinking it was normal, and seeing your friends and other family members going through the same thing thinking that this type of living is just what everyone goes through. That is until you go to that one person's house that opens your eyes to show you no! In fact, no one lives like that -- only the ones who choose and accept that way of living.

Even with that awakening, seeing that you do have a better choice of living. Some will still choose to be held down by the hands of their own oppression. Never realizing their full potential. Having a job is never a bad thing, but you must also realize that as long as you work under someone, they will never let you move over them. Your hard work is accredited to the person with the higher position. That didn't even lift a finger to help with the actual task and eventually gets the raise that you truthfully deserve. When they do give you a raise, it's only between 25 cents and 1 dollar. And you are happy to take that, because you are just getting by as it is, and every dollar counts, right? No one will ever pay you like you pay yourself and only you can find your worth. You can never expect someone to let you succeed higher than they are because their success is based off of your success but if you focus on your own there is no way for them to place an option on how to ensure your place on the never ending trail of mediocrity.

CHAPTER 4
UNTAPPED POTENTIAL

So many people have so many talents and abilities, but lack the proper motivation or even know how to utilize their abilities. Everyone wants to be rich or well off, but lack the self-motivation and willpower to get out and make it happen for themselves. There is a saying that says, "Nothing comes easy" and it is very true. The hardest thing is just to get started. Once it is in motion, it is hard to stop depending on yourself and your will, to make a life change and keep the change for the betterment of yourself and your family.

The most obvious symptoms and most sensitive to the ears of the ones with untapped potential is flat out laziness. Lazy is probably one of the most controversial words in the human language, mainly because it is letting a person know they are not putting the effort that they know they possess and giving a full 100 percent. People who have problems with confidence will let their laziness get the best of them. The mindset they develop through being lazy gives a sense of self-satisfaction in its own. It is negatively affecting your future to become the best that you are and can be.

Sometimes it is not others blocking your path to success it is truly yourself and only by realizing, what your worth is from within will you be able to make other see your worth from the outside. Finding a purpose has been one of the biggest wonders of human nature and truly, only you can look from within to find that exact cause and excel in every aspect of what you believe is set in stone for you. I believe in you, so why not believe in yourself. Having a system of support set up around you that encourages you to go outside your comfort zone, and do things outside of the normal will help you become the person you want to be. When engaging yourself in the quest for self-motivation, the first thing you must do is believe, that you have the potential to be one of the greatest to ever do it. With this in mind, no one can tell you that, what you want to do cannot be done, but instead you can show them that you on the contrary, we're built for these type of things.

CHAPTER 5
DEBT AND CREDIT

All too often, so many of us get caught up in the hype of life, forget to take a look at the future. By the time you blink, you are 30. With a $40,000-school loan, a sketchy car loan, and two apartment evictions on your credit report. One thing that is not taught very much, not only in the black community but every ethnically diverse community, is credit.

It is very seldom that the value of credit is taught. If ever, and if you happen to learn about it in college, you would have had to take a class major in that subject. This system has been the same for decades now and does not seem to be changing any time soon. Without a way to teach the next generation how to advance, the cycle continues.

Generations upon generations subjugated into a lack of knowledge, about the things that really decipher the difference in having a productive future and having a never-ending cycle of debt and interest on debt. What they do not teach is how easy it is to accumulate debt. As simple as signing your name on a piece of paper can have you in the proverbial hole for practically your entire life. Possibly be passed onto your kids who definitely do not deserve to inherit that type of financial stress.

There are many ways to prevent yourself from falling into these traps but it is going to take more than a vigilante eye to do so. You will need the mental knowledge to know what you are looking for. The things that are presented may not always appear, as it seems. You can think you are getting that nice car you always wanted but in the fine print, it states that you do not actually pay the amount that you originally intended to pay. In fact, the increase that was in fine print makes the car completely out of budget but you have signed the papers; legally law-binding papers, that these "lenders" will not hesitate to take you to court for. Without the legalities, it's loan sharking without the violence. It takes for the person to actually go through these struggles to completely understand, instead of taking the previous person that went through that very thing that could have been avoided if only taught the right way.

CHAPTER 6
BUDGET AND SPENDING

What do people love to do more than making money? Spending it of course! Some are not even aware of the spending habits that they have it does not necessarily have to be branded clothes and expensive cars. Simply having to go to the store for one thing at a time, instead of buying in bulk.

All too often, we live in the now, where the future is not as important. Now, I am not saying you do not feel like your future has potential. I am saying you would rather spend 1.99 on an eight pack of angel soft, than spend 8.99 on a pack of 36 Charmin double size rolls. At that moment, you are thinking that you could have saved five, but really, you are spending five extra just to go back to the store when you need more tissue paper. Except, the second time, you are using more gas and getting tax one extra time. Both which you could have prevented.

That is just a simple analogy of basic spending habits and the inability of controlling impulses to buy things in the now. There can be the opposites as well; where you overspend just because you "got it", and you know the routine. Your check is 1000, but your bills for this check is 600. So you feel you have 400 to spend, when in reality you put yourself in the hole even before you got paid... sad but true. This is called over budgeting where you spend all that you make or even more than you were able to make.

This form of spending is applicable to all shopping. From overpriced clothing to a high phone bill or car note.

Not being able to see into your spending habits can be ruinous to the growth of your financial freedom. Under budgeting can be just as crippling when it comes to the common goal of being financially stable. How, you ask? Having the ability to choose the things you WANT to buy is a luxury compared to having the ability to buy the things you NEED and being able to understand the distinct difference between the two. Having gas in your car to commute to generate revenue, is something you need. Having gas in the car to go to the store and to get fast food is something you want, but do not necessarily need. There is a very fine line when trying to make the Judgment of what you think is important opposed to what you know becoming more financially aware.

CHAPTER 7
SOCIAL STATUS

In many cases, and all too often, people tend to go broke trying to keep up with the Joneses, or for a more modern trend, "Keeping up with the Kardashians". This problem is more like an illness of the brain than distress in the wallet. Having a persona where you are mainly judged by your image is very tough. If you are not trying to outdo the next big outfit you wore, you definitely want to try to outdo the last. It's never a bad thing to want to look good but it's a lot different when you are no longer looking for self-satisfaction but the credibility and approval of other's opinions.

Impressions, which really does not matter in the end when you figure out only your judgment matters. Portraying rich or well off, instead of getting rich, is really the downfall of the fast life and socially inept. They think looking a certain way will gain social acceptability from anyone who will give it. Ironically, the "liking" is only reciprocated in person. As soon as you walk away, it's another story and no one has the same support for you.

Being able to choose the right people to be around, that you know will elevate you to the next level, should be priority number one, when deciphering what type of crowd you want to be around you. There is a saying, "If you are the smartest person in your group, find a new group". I personally loved this, because if your peers are not intellectually challenging you, then you will never reach the pinnacle of your intellectual intelligence.

CHAPTER 8
PEOPLE PLEASER

People will spend their last on another person before they spend it on themselves, thinking that it will come back to them "in the long run" from the very person they help. When in reality the thought of payback or restitution has not even crossed their minds.

One thing about being a people pleaser is that you never put yourself first and that in itself cannot strive financially. Having a job that has a very good pay can cripple your mind into thinking that you have an abundance of money. That you can part with it without affecting bills and rent. That is the disadvantage of giving your last because you do not feel it is really your last, yet you feel more assured you could get it back. It takes a lot for a person that has always thought of others before themselves to change suddenly, but without the mindset of self-wealth and self-worth, the primary goal of trying to obtain financial freedom will never come to fruition.

By neglecting to place your needs of wanting for nothing and asserting your willingness to give will never have the outcome that you wished for only the outcome come that you place for others to make sure that they are good.

CHAPTER 9
RAINY DAY FUNDS

Even when a person has money coming in on a regular, tend to forget about the rainy day funds. What are these rainy day funds, you ask?

Consider how many times, just the slightest inconvenience, in going over budget; even if it's in paying bills normally and miscalculating can put you in the preverbal "hole". So, imagine how hard it's going to be when that oil change turns into a blown gasket, or your home insurance doesn't cover that Arizona heat in the dead of the summer for a quick ac fix. Imagine living a single bachelor/bachelorette lifestyle. Then all the sudden, a baby comes into play. One of the first thoughts that come to mind is finances and how you're going to be able to afford what's been put on your plate. That's why it's always good to think about the unexpected and not only think about it but also prepare for it. The last thing you want is to be in your mid 30s trying to teach your child how to struggle but in a more efficient way.

Sadly this has been our mindset for past generations but you can be the one to stop this ongoing trend in your family and community. It takes a lot for a person to build that tolerance against frivolous spending but once you can set your mind to that one aspect of setting a foundation for future occurrences that can happen to anyone, you will soon find out how many opportunities open.

Preparing for not only yourself but if you have a family should always be top priority so having some type of financial assurance will always be a good look for everyone's benefit, invest in yourself and always look forward to the future of the expecting the unexpected.

CHAPTER 10
SOCIAL LIFE

Everyone, well not everyone but most, love to have a good time and a large portion of the time it cost to do so, which is not a problem but when it becomes a weekly event of large spending you rarely notice it because of the great times your having. That's is until you check your bank account and notice those two extra patron shots and 5 tacos from jack in the box really cost more than you thought, truthfully lots of us have been through the let me check to see what I bought dilemma checking and calculating all your past transactions when you could have avoided the unnecessary spending before it took place. Some don't have the financial struggles problems as much but still find themselves spending more than they would like and sometimes it's not on yourself sometimes it's spending for your "friends" a boyfriend or girlfriends that doesn't really have your best interests at heart and just want to have a good time with you that really cost them nothing. This especially when it comes to the social verbally inept it's a lot more easy for the friend to dictate the amount of money they spend which often is usually until they have no money to spend. Being able to keep an open mind to misguided social spending can be the first guide to really investing in yourself to better your situation and hopefully the ones around you as well, all it takes is a bit of motivation determination and perseverance and you can become the person you always wanted to be remember no one will take care of you like yourself.

CHAPTER 11
DISORGANIZATION

Not having a set plan can be so detrimental to having the financial freedom that you long for, being organized and having a sound plan will always have the best turn out. You wouldn't put together an engine and feel safe using it without a set plan so why treat your life any different, in some ways you have to look at your life as the business that you want to run and always make sure that is in order. How can you lead a shift if you're not the leader of your own shift? How can I begin being more organized you ask yourself? maybe picking up a few extra things around the house on the regular or setting a wash schedule for the clothes some would put a weekly amount of extra cash away to invest truth is any start is better than no start and that's the first step in the Path to Progression in your life. When you have a dream and want to see it played out before your eyes you should feel like you would do anything to make that happen but without a plan you just have a vision or a mirage which only an illusion, a figment of what your real agenda is it should always be in your plans to stay on target with what you strive for and knowing that without having organization and dedication with a devoted loyal attitude everything will be that much more difficult.

CHAPTER 12
OVER NIGHT SUCCESS

Some have it figured out almost to a point of excellence they have a plan to create their financial stabilization but lack the patience to see it through. Thinking you can start a business and get the money you invested back overnight your very mistaken in how making investments work, overnight success is a phrase from the movies made up in Hollywood to give the false hope that you can make a million over night some don't necessarily expect reimbursement so quickly but they definitely don't expect to wait two to three years to start making an actual profit which can been very frustrating at times and even discouraging but time and patience is all you need to be successful especially when making long term investments like building a business, company or brand. Having more than one thing that you invest in is vital when trying to make a way for you to have financial stability and eventually financial freedom everything that you invest in doesn't necessarily have to relate either. You can have money dabbling in art and design as well as in the stock market you can invest in investing there are so many different avenues for you to create a steady flow of revenue it just takes the time for you to do the research and have the ambition within yourself to find theses ways to do so.

CHAPTER 13
ROLE MODELS

Having the right role models can be just as important as the circle that you keep around you in fact it should actually dictate the way you choose the people in your circle. Wanting to surround yourself with likeminded people is vital when creating a path to Progression, everyone has heard the saying you hang around 5 bums you going to be the 6th to start in that very same trend but surrounding yourself with motivation and financial longevity it will only end one way and that's with Success. Always be cautious of the company you keep everyone doesn't have your best interest in mind and only want to be around when it's beneficial for them, having role models that you see at clubs and partying on TV can influence the feeling of wanting to be needed to feel important hence surrounding themselves with others that provide no productivity to their lives. Having a role model doesn't always have to be someone doing something that you've seen on TV and doesn't necessarily have to be a person in fact it can be owning a Business as a goal or a position goal such as CEO of a corporation maybe even starting off small on a small scale is better than not starting at all the primary goal is to never be stagnant and always move forward and having the right person or people to look up to can be nothing but a plus in helping you complete your agenda.

ABOUT THE AUTHOR

Author Lance Ott gives a look at what it took for him to become the passionate financially motivated person that you see and hear about today. Going through every imaginable obstacle there is not much that he has not gone through giving him the realization that we are all more alike than we think.

www.ingramcontent.com/pod-product-compliance
Lightning Source LLC
Chambersburg PA
CBHW070828220526
45466CB00002B/778